For my mini-me, Meera Asha,

and all the STEM girls out there!

www.mascotbooks.com

Elara, STEM Girl

For more information, please contact:
Mascot Books
620 Herndon Parkway #320
Herndon, VA 20170
info@mascotbooks.com

Library of Congress Control Number: 2018903513

CPSIA Code: PRT0518A
ISBN-13: 978-1-68401-676-1

Printed in the United States

ELARA,
STEM GIRL

By Leela Ayyar

Hi, my name is Elara. In case you didn't know, that's the name of a moon of Jupiter but I like to be called STEM Girl!

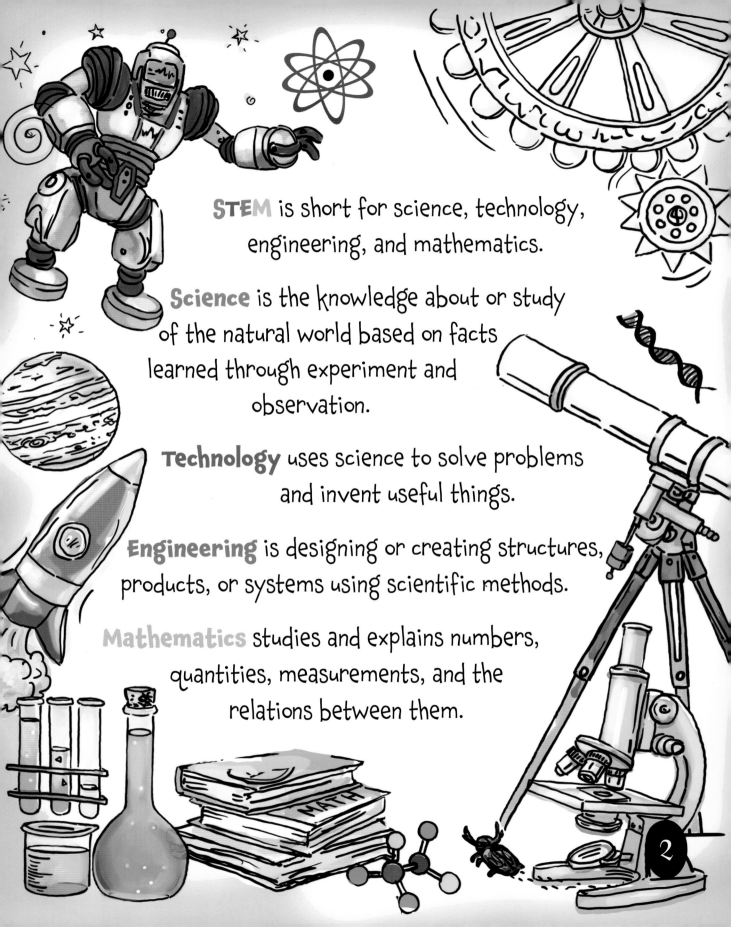

STEM is short for science, technology, engineering, and mathematics.

Science is the knowledge about or study of the natural world based on facts learned through experiment and observation.

Technology uses science to solve problems and invent useful things.

Engineering is designing or creating structures, products, or systems using scientific methods.

Mathematics studies and explains numbers, quantities, measurements, and the relations between them.

I'm like a lot of girls you know. I like dolls, dress-up, and sports, but I really *love* STEM!

Now that my older brother is a teenager, he doesn't play with a lot of his toys anymore. So, they are all mine! I use them to engineer buildings, create inventions, and investigate my world.

"All sorts of things can happen when you're open to new ideas and playing around with things." — Stephanie Kwolek, Chemist

Many of the girls I know aren't interested in STEM. I think it's because they don't know how fun it can be! They're missing out!

People have their own ideas about the toys I should and shouldn't play with. Dressing up dolls and having a tea party is fun, but building a fort or looking at things under a magnifying glass is awesome!

7

"Do not let others define who you are. Define yourself. Do not be limited by what others expect of you, but reach confidently for the stars." – Shirley Ann Jackson, Physicist

My mom and dad have always encouraged me to do my best no matter what interests me.

I used to think I wasn't good at math, so I never answered any questions in class. But then my dad told me that no one is born good at math.

It just takes practice! It's no different from piano or soccer. You have to practice! So I practiced and practiced... Now, I'm the best mathematician in my class!

In social studies we rarely talk about women scientists or inventors. Here are some of my favorites!

I've made it a personal goal to learn about as many as possible!

One of my favorite after-school activities is Robotics Club, where I build, design, and play with robots!

At first, I felt uncomfortable since I'm the only girl in the club, but that all went away when I started designing my robot. Building something and watching it work is the best feeling!

"I didn't succumb to the stereotype that science wasn't for girls." – Sally Ride, Physicist and Astronaut

Sometimes my robot doesn't work as expected, but as Einstein said, "You never fail until you stop trying."

So, I keep reprograming it over and over until it performs the task perfectly.

"Above all, don't fear difficult moments. The best comes from them." — Rita-Levi Montalcini, Neurologist

Every time robotics class meets, I make new friends. I imagine I'm just like Sally Ride and other women who paved the way for girls in science. I can't wait to greet the next girl who signs up for robotics club!

My birthday is coming up, so my mom and I are planning my party. But everything in the party store "girl" aisle was princess-themed! I like princesses but how many princess parties can one girl have?

Then I had a creative idea! I'll have a STEM-themed party with activities based on each STEM topic!

"Never be limited by other people's limited imaginations."
— Mae Jemison, Engineer, Physician, and Astronaut

After much analysis*, I've decided on four activities that I know will show my friends how much fun STEM can be.

S: make your own slime

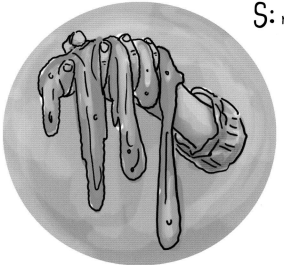

T: technology scavenger hunt

E: build your own catapult and marshmallow launch contest

M: musical math

Analysis is a sciencey word for a careful study of something after considering everything possible

The day of my party is finally here! My friends had tons of fun, and learned a lot too! Who knew you could launch a marshmallow ten feet in the air using only jumbo popsicle sticks?

I took my robot out for a spin at my party to show my friends what I engineered in robotics club. They were impressed!

My STEM party was a huge success. At the next robotics class, several girls were there too!

Now we can be STEM girls together!

"It is invaluable to have a friend who shares your interests and helps you stay motivated." – Maryam Mirzakhani, Mathematician

Stephanie Kwolek

Chemist

She is best known for inventing the first of a family of synthetic fibers that would become Kevlar. For her discovery, Kwolek was the first woman to be awarded the DuPont Company's Lavoisier Medal for outstanding technical achievement. Kwolek also received the National Medal of Technology, IRI Achievement Award, Perkin Medal, and was inducted into the National Inventors Hall of Fame.

Shirley Ann Jackson

Physicist

She was the first African-American woman to receive a doctorate from MIT in any field and the first to lead a national research university (Rensselaer). Dr. Jackson was awarded the National Medal of Science, the nation's highest honor for contributions in science and engineering.

Marie Curie

Physicist and Chemist

She conducted pioneering research on radioactivity, discovering polonium and radium. She was the first woman to win a Nobel Prize, and the first person and only woman to win this prestigious award twice in two different sciences. Curie was also the first woman to become a professor at the University of Paris.

Sally Ride

Physicist and Astronaut

She was the first American woman in space. Dr. Ride received numerous honors and awards. She was inducted into the National Women's Hall of Fame and the Astronaut Hall of Fame.

Rita-Levi Montalcini

Neurologist

She was awarded the Nobel Prize in Physiology or Medicine in 1986 jointly with colleague Stanley Cohen for the discovery of nerve growth factor (NGF). Montalcini also served in the Italian Senate as a Senator for Life and received the National Medal of Science.

Mae Jemison

Physician, Engineer, and Astronaut

She was the first African-American woman to travel in space when she went into orbit aboard the Space Shuttle Endeavour on September 12, 1992. She was inducted into the National Women's Hall of Fame and the International Space Hall of Fame.

Maryam Mirzakhani

Mathematician

She was the first woman and Iranian to be awarded the Fields Medal, the discipline's most celebrated prize, "for her outstanding contributions to the dynamics and geometry of Riemann surfaces and their moduli spaces."

Go to www.ElaraSTEMGirl.com
to download additional experiment cards,
Elara's party games, and find tons of STEM girl activities.

Definitions from Merriam-Webster's Advanced Learner's English Dictionary ©2017 by Merriam-Webster, Inc.

SOURCES

American Physical Society www.aps.org
Encyclopedia Britannica www.britannica.com
NASA www.nasa.gov
National Women's Hall of Fame www.womenofthehall.org
The official website of the Nobel Prize www.nobelprize.org
Quotes from AZQuotes.com and SigmaXI.org

Acknowledgments

There are so many people who helped make this book possible. First, a special thanks to my family and friends. My mom, Kristin Ayyar, who is the reason this book became a reality, and my best friend, Shannen Prindle, for the wonderful Kickstarter video and for always being a nerd with me. And a huge thank you to all my Kickstarter backers who believed in this project and its importance! In particular, thank you Angeles de Leon, Colleen Eddy, Margaret and Frank Della Pia, and Rakesh Mathur for your generous support.

About the Author

Growing up, Leela Ayyar had always been fascinated with the night sky. Her love for the stars quickly expanded to all of the sciences as she grew up. Inspired by the challenges she and her younger sister experienced as STEM girls, Leela wrote *Elara, STEM Girl* to not only encourage girls to take an interest in STEM but to help them overcome any obstacle they may face!